behind the yew hedge

drawings by Mathew Staunton
haiku & senryu by Gabriel Rosenstock

The Onslaught Press

Published in Oxford by The Onslaught Press
11 Ridley Road, OX4 2QJ
September, 2016

Texts © 2016 **Gabriel Rosenstock**

Cover, illustrations, & this edition © 2016 **Mathew Staunton**

Mathew Staunton & Gabriel Rosenstock assert their moral right
to be identified as the authors of this book

All rights reserved. No part of this publication may be reproduced, stored
in a retrieval system, or transmitted, in any form or by any means,
electronic, mechanical, photocopying, recording, or
otherwise, without the prior permission in writing of the publisher,
or as expressly permitted by law, or under terms agreed with the
appropriate reprographics rights organization

ISBN: **978-0-9956225-8-6**

Designed and typeset in **DIN Next** by Mathew Staunton

Printed by Lightning Source

for Aoife & Finn

boladh muisc—
seanlitreacha grá
doléite nach mór

musky odour—
old love letters
almost illegible

alien abduction—
birdsong no longer
the same

**fuadach eachtardhomhanda—
cantaireacht éan
ní hé an rud céanna é**

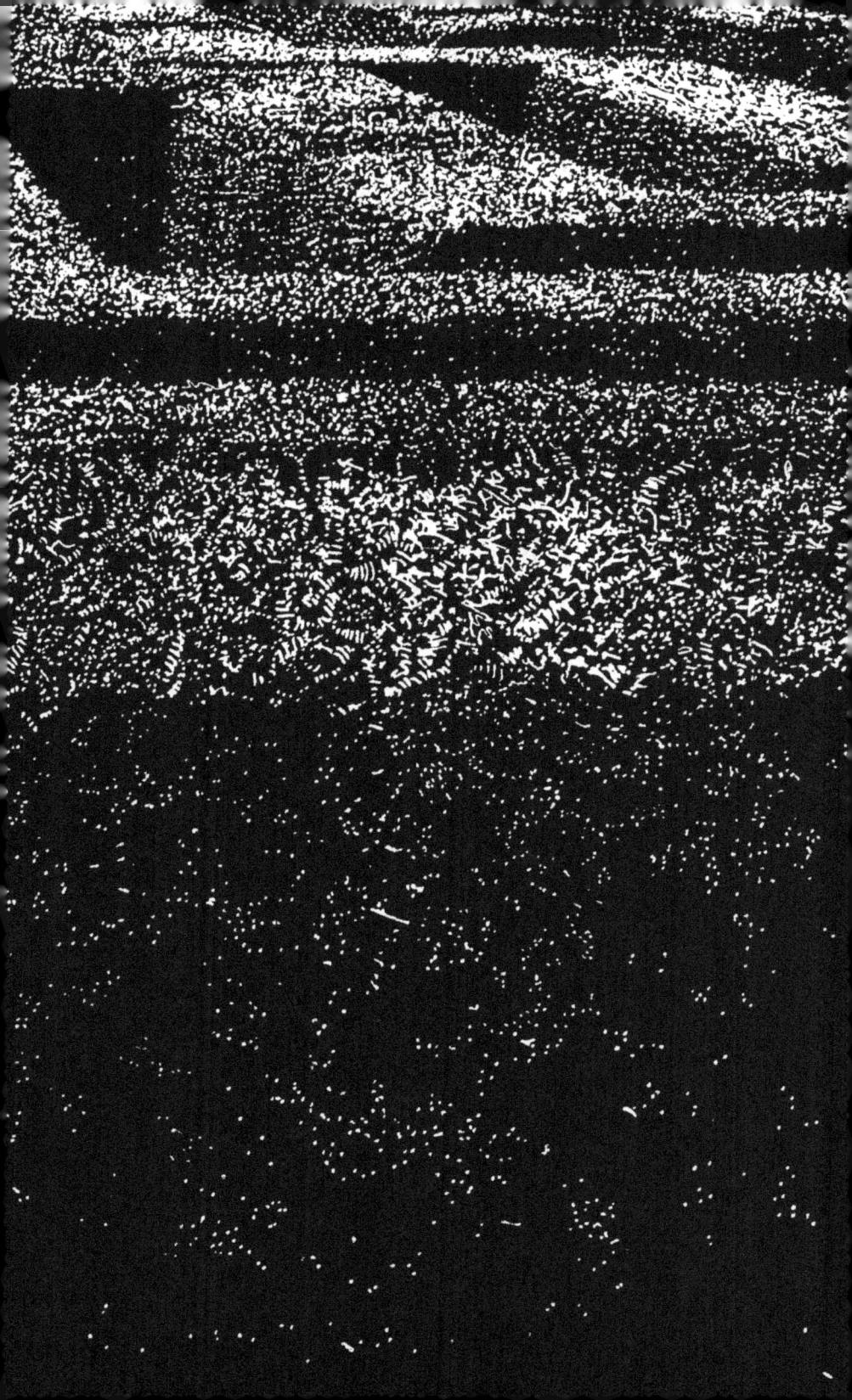

braon báistí . . .
cuimhne gan choinne
ar dheora dé i gciarraí

a drop of rain . . .
suddenly remembering
fuchsia in kerry

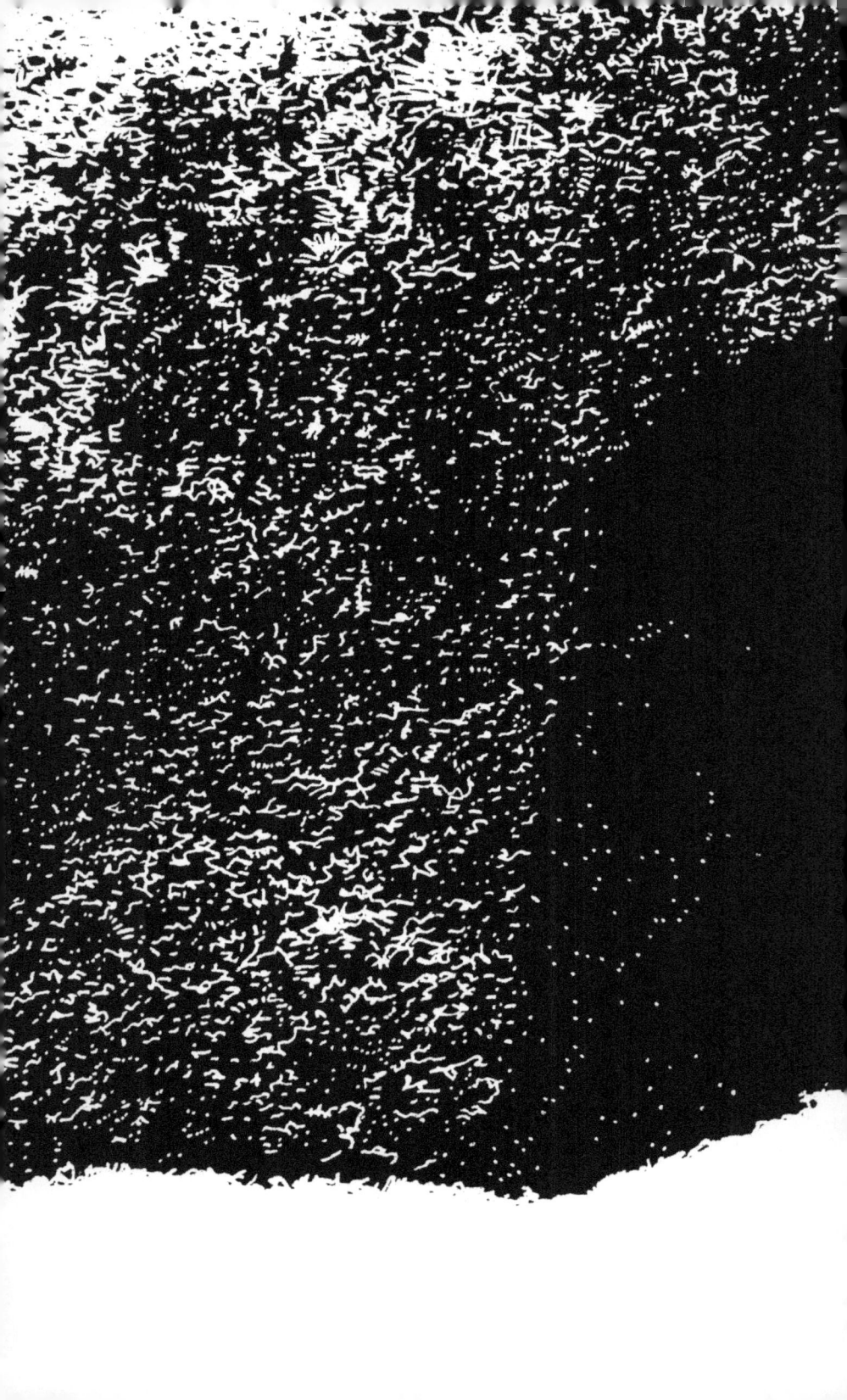

domhnach tais—
imirce na scamall
arís inniu

damp sunday—
the emigration of clouds
again today

mug of green tea . . .
slowly the hands
grow warm

muga tae ghlais . . .
teas sna lámha
de réir a chéile

cruicéad
ar an raidió—
preabann spideog chuig craobhóg eile

cricket
on the radio—
a robin hops to another twig

leanaí ag súgradh—
scáthanna scáthanna
gach aon áit

children at play—
shadows shadows
everywhere

binse páirce—
fear an phoist ar scor
ag bogchaoineadh

park bench—
a retired postman
sobs quietly

poetry & haiku titles from The Onslaught Press

Out of the Wilderness (2016) by Cathal Ó Searcaigh
with an introduction and translations by Gabriel Rosenstock

You Found a Beating Heart (2016) Nisha Bhakoo

ident (2016) Alan John Stubbs

I Wanna Make Jazz to You (2016) Moe Seager

Tea wi the Abbot (2016) Scots haiku by John McDonald
with transcreations in Irish by Gabriel Rosenstock

Judgement Day (2016) Gabriel Rosenstock

We Want Everything (2016) Moe Seager

to kingdom come (2016) edited by Rethabile Masilo

The Lost Box of Eyes (2016) Alan John Stubbs

Antlered Stag of Dawn (2015) Gabriel Rosenstock,
with translations by Mariko Sumikura & John McDonald

behind the yew hedge (2015) Mathew Staunton & Gabriel Rosenstock

Bumper Cars (2015) Athol Williams

Waslap (2015) Rethabile Masilo

Aistear Anama (2014) Tadhg Ó Caoinleáin

for the children of Gaza (2014)
edited by Mathew Staunton & Rethabile Masilo

Poison Trees (2014) Philippe Saltel & Mathew Staunton

www.ingramcontent.com/pod-product-compliance
Lightning Source LLC
Chambersburg PA
CBHW051720040426
42446CB00008B/978